T0117178

海拔以上的情感: 商禽散文詩選

Feelings Above Sea Level
Prose Poems from the Chinese of
Shang Qin

TRANSLATED BY STEVE BRADBURY

ZEPHYR PRESS
Brookline, MA

Chinese Copyright © 2006 by Shang Qin
Translation, Preface & Notes Copyright © 2006 by Steve Bradbury
All rights reserved.

Cover drawing and interior art by Shang Qin
Book design by *typeslowly*
Printed in Michigan by Cushing-Malloy, Inc.

Zephyr Press acknowledges with gratitude the financial support
of the Massachusetts Cultural Council and the National Endowment
for the Arts.

NATIONAL
ENDOWMENT
FOR THE ARTS

massculturalcouncil.org

Zephyr Press, a non-profit arts and education 501(c)(3) organization,
publishes literary titles that foster deeper understanding of cultures and
languages. Zephyr books are distributed to the trade in the U.S. and Canada
by Consortium Book Sales and Distribution [www.cbsd.com] and by Small
Press Distribution [www.spdbooks.org].

Library of Congress Cataloging-in-Publication Data

Luo, Yan, 1930-
  [Poems. English. Selections]
  Feelings above sea level : prose poems from the Chinese of Shang Qin ;
translated by Steve Bradbury.
     p. cm.
  Includes bibliographical references and index.
  ISBN 0-939010-89-5 (alk. paper)
  I. Bradbury, Steve. II. Title.
  PL2880.O3664A24 2006
  895.6'15--dc22

                          2006024295

98765432 first edition in 2006

ZEPHYR PRESS
50 Kenwood Street
Brookline, MA 02446
www.zephyrpress.org

Grateful acknowledgment is made to the editors of the following publications in which many of these translations first appeared: *Chinese Pen (Taiwan)*, *Cipher Journal*, *Circumference*, *Double Room*, *eXchanges*, *Fascicle*, *Full Tilt*, *Sentence: A Journal of Prose Poetics*, *Tinfish*, *Trout*, and *Valley Voices: A Literary Review*.

Table of Contents

Translator's Preface

Shang Qin 商禽 was born in Sichuan, China in 1930, but has lived in Taiwan since the late Forties. The author of four volumes of poetry, he is among the first poets in Taiwan to have expressed a significant interest in surrealism and is the finest poet writing in Chinese on either side of the Formosa Strait to have made the prose poem his métier.

Many literary critics and scholars have described the bizarre circumstances under which this now 76-year-old poet first encountered prose poetry in 1945 at the ripe age of fifteen, but no account is more engaging than the one the poet himself provides in the preface to the revised edition of his first volume of verse, *Dream or the Dawn and Other* (夢或著黎明及其他):

> The year I turned 15, I was press-ganged by soldiers of Chiang Kai-shek's Nationalist Army in the streets of Chengdu and locked up in an old barn of a warehouse. After a week's incarceration I was pretty much broken in, but I discovered the place was filled with books the like of which I'd never seen before. This was my first exposure to what we then called the "New Literature." It was there I read Lu Xun's *Wild Grass* and Bing Xin's *Stars* [two seminal works in the genealogy of the Chinese prose poem].

After a month, I set out with the troops for Chongqing [Chiang Kai-shek's stronghold during the war against Japan], but before we got there I managed to engineer the first of many escapes in my fugitive existence. Even now I can vividly recall the lights of the fishing boats on the Jialing River and the murmur of the water as it flows to the sea.... My intention was to return to my family home in Sichuan, but I was captured by one troop detachment after another only to escape each time. In total, I must have run away at least half a dozen times and in the process tramped through every nook and corner of southern China without ever reaching my destination ...

In the end, however, the Nationalist troops that caught me last were forced to engineer their own escape to Taiwan and took me with them. There I found the linguistic barriers to communication and the trivial distances between towns and villages took all the pleasure out of flight. Before long I no longer had the physical energy to run away, and I found the only escape left me was to flee from one name into another. But no matter how many times I changed my name, I could not escape from myself ... and thus it is I am ever caught on the verge of dream or the dawn.

The poet finally settled on the penname Shang Qin (a homonym for "wounded bird" 傷禽) and began publishing poetry in the mid-Fifties in various modernist journals such as *Modern Poetry Quarterly* 現代詩 (*Xiandai shi*) while still employed as a soldier. He was not discharged from the military until 1968 and spent the next two years attending the International Writing Program at the University of Iowa before returning to Taiwan, where he tried his hand at a host of trades from street vendor and gardener to bookstore clerk and editor. He eventually became associate chief-editor of the *China Times Weekly* 中國時報週刊 (*Zhongguo shibao zhoukan*) and retired in 1992.

Shang Qin's reputation as a prose poet was slow in maturing and did not really take wing until the appearance of his first volume of poetry *Dream or the Dawn*, which he published the year he left for Iowa. In the mid-Thirties, when the island was still under Japanese colonial rule and Taiwan's poets looked to Japan rather than to China for poetic inspiration, a few aspiring modernists who had studied in the "Empire of the Sun" and wrote in the Japanese language, briefly experimented with prose poetry, which had been in vogue in Japan since the early Twenties. In the Forties and early Fifties, after Taiwan once again came under Chinese political and cultural influence, a handful of poets, most prominently Ji Xian 紀弦, began writing prose poems in Chinese. However, few of these early ventures in the form are particularly impressive and none as accomplished as the prose poems Shang Qin began publishing in the late Fifties.

Although most critics describe Shang Qin as a surrealist poet, this attribution is somewhat problematic. To be sure, surrealism has had considerable influence on the poet's work. Much of his early poetry has that eerie "dream logic" associated with surrealism, and several of his poems were clearly inspired by seminal works in the European surrealist tradition, as seen in the poem "My Amoeba Kid Brother," which directly alludes to and plays off of Joan Miró's celebrated 1926 painting "Dog Barking at the Moon," and the more recent "Moonlight," which is awash with allusions to Max Jacob's prose poem "The Truly Miraculous." At the same time, one cannot help noting that, in the mid-Eighties, when the Nationalist Government began relaxing its surveillance of the nation's writers in anticipation of the end of martial law, much of Shang Qin's surrealism falls from the bone, so to speak. Which suggests that surrealism may have been a political cover for the poet of compassion and social justice that one only glimpsed now and then in Shang Qin's earlier work, but who emerges fully in 1987 when the end of martial law brought an end to government censorship. While this transformation is most conspicuous in the political elegies Shang Qin published over the next few years, such as "The Speed of Sound," which is dedicated to a victim of police brutality during the martial law period, and "Snow, June, 1989," which the poet wrote in response to the Tiananmen Square Massacre, his compassion is evident in the lion's share of poems published since 1987.

Since the purpose of the present volume is to showcase the quality of the poet's work in this particular genre rather than to present a comprehensive survey of his oeuvre, I have limited my translations to those prose poems that have lent themselves to translation into English. In some cases, the differences between the Chinese and English languages and poetic traditions have compelled me to augment the translation of a title or a phrase in the poem proper to convey the force or significance of the original poem. I have indicated these departures in my notes, and have included additional notes for the poems whose literary sources and/ or informing contexts may be of interest to readers.

I am grateful to the following friends and fellow travelers for their suggestions and encouragement: Lisa Rose Bradford, Tim Casey, Stuart Hopen, Jerome Li, Wenchi Lin, Silvia Marijnissen, Zona Yi-ping Tsou, Lily Wong, and, last but not least, Shang Qin, to whom I am also grateful for allowing Zephyr Press to reproduce the drawings included in this volume.

Feelings Above Sea Level

火雞

一個小孩告訴我：那火雞要在吃東西時才把鼻上的肉綬收縮起來；挺挺地，像一個角。我就想；火雞也不是喜歡說閒話的家禽；而它所啼出來的僅僅是些抗議，而已。

蓬著翅羽的火雞很像孔雀；（連它的鳴聲也像，為此，我曾經傷心過。）但孔雀乃炫耀它的美——由於寂寞；而火雞則往往是在示威——向著虛無。

向虛無示威的火雞，並不懂形而上學。

喜歡吃富有葉綠素的蔥尾。

談戀愛，而很少同戀人散步。

也思想，常常，但都不是我們所能懂的。

The Turkey

A child once pointed out to me that it's only when a turkey eats that its snood stiffens up like a horn. Which got me thinking that the turkey is not one of your run-of-the-mill domestic fowl with a fondness for idle chatter. Indeed, its every cry is nothing if not a protest.

When it ruffles up its feathers the turkey bears an amazing resemblance to the peacock. (It even sounds the same, the thought of which once filled me with grief.) But while the peacock flaunts its splendor out of feelings of loneliness, the turkey ruffles up in an unending effort to put on a show of force in the face of nothingness.

A turkey that puts on a show of force in the face of nothingness clearly has a feeble grasp of metaphysics.

It likes to eat the chlorophyll-rich tips of the scallion.

It lightly turns its thoughts to love but rarely takes a stroll with its significant other.

It also thinks, quite often, but hardly the sort of thoughts we could ever understand.

天使們的惡作劇

當人們看見了那祗是一窩赤裸裸的連眼也不曾睜開的鼠嬰之後，我被他們所投擲的酒瓶埋葬之時，我知道這是無可解釋的了；只好把我的信念噓進每一個瓶口：我確曾見得那是一堆各種族類的張著翅膀的但是閉著眼的美麗的鳥屍；至於一窩鼠嬰，我想，這一定是天使們的惡作劇。知道嗎？天使們的惡作劇。

The Angels' Idea of a Practical Joke

When everyone saw only a litter of baby mice, naked and pink, that had never even opened their eyes, I knew, lying under the mound of their discarded liquor bottles, I knew that this defied all reason, knew that there was nothing I could do but breathe my slender faith down the throat of each bottle. For I'd seen these were in fact the dead bodies of various species of beautiful birds, with wings poised as if for flight but eyes closed forever on the world. As for the litter of mice, that must, I think, have been the angels' idea of a practical joke. You know what I mean? The angels' idea of a practical joke.

流質

逃避了秋的初次搜索的一條夏天的尾巴躲在候車室內，把一個女子催眠爲流質了。所有的男人都很惋惜；他們的眼睛都說：「完了！這可憐的，可愛的女子。她再也不能把自已和她的夢撿起來了，甚至用湯匙也不能…」而我卻暗自歡喜。我想：「如果我能在這些液體還沒有被蒸發之前得到一張上等的棉紙就好了。我可以把那浮在面表的鉛粉以及口紅拓印下來，這樣，我在死後就有遺產了…」若非突來一股冷風將我冷卻，我也已經融爲液體了。

Liquid

Fleeing from the first autumn sweep, the tail end of summer holed up in a station waiting room, where it hypnotized a woman until she turned to liquid. All the men in the waiting room felt very sorry for her and their eyes seemed to say: "Well, you can sure kiss that one goodbye! What a pity, she was such a pretty thing. She'll never pick herself up now, or her dreams, even with a spoon."

But I was secretly pleased and could not help thinking, "If I can only get my hands on a sheet of high-quality rag paper before she evaporates and make a rubbing of the lipstick smears and facial powder floating in the puddle of her, I'll finally have a little something to leave in my will." And if a sudden blast of cold air hadn't cooled me down, I'd have turned to liquid too.

海拔以上的情感

雨季開始以後，兀鷹們不再在谷空吹他們令人心悸的口哨了。

怎麼你想起一隻退休的船；海蠔浮雕著舵，肆無忌憚地豪笑的魚群空手歸去；而一隻粗心的老鼠在兩年后醒來躺在甲板上哭了。其實你是一隻現役的狗。雨天不一定是聖餐日。慈悲的印度王子不會給你一隻他的香港腳。而獵風的人回來，得到的僅僅是一個紅色的乳鐘形的鼻子…

等晚上吧，我將逃亡，沿拾薪者的小徑，上到山頂；這裏的夜好自私，連半片西瓜皮都沒有；卻用我不曾流出的淚，將香檳酒色的星子們擊得粉碎。

Feelings Above Sea Level

After the rains came, the emptiness of the valley no longer rang with the fearful cries of the Griffon vultures.

How did you come to think of a rusticated boat? Oysters make relief sculptures of the rudder, as schools of fish, roaring with brazen laughter, head home empty-handed, as a careless rat that woke up two years after lies weeping on the deck. In point of fact you are a dog on active duty. A rainy day is not perforce a Maundy Thursday. The compassionate Kashmiri prince will not offer you the leg with athlete's foot. But the hunter of winds returns, with nothing to show for his pains but a crimson nose in the shape of the nippled-bell at Fangshan Dinglin Temple ...

Wait until evening, when I shall make my escape and follow the narrow path of the firewood gatherers up to the mountaintop. How selfish the night is here. Not a sliver of watermelon rind to spare, yet it will use the tears I haven't even shed to smash the champagne-colored stars to smithereens.

界

據說有戰爭在遠方 . . .

於此，微明時的大街，有巡警被阻於一毫無
障礙之某處。無何，乃負手，垂頭，踱著方
步；想解釋，想尋出：「界」在哪裏；因而
爲此一意圖所雕塑。

而爲一隻野狗所目睹的，一條界，乃由晨起
的漱洗者凝視的目光，所射出昨夜夢境趨勢
之覺與折自一帶水泥磚牆頂的玻璃頭髮的回
聲所織成。

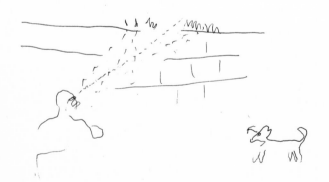

Border Zone

They say that war is raging in a distant land ...

And so, on a certain avenue in the wee hours of the night a watchman on his rounds suddenly found his forward motion checked at a place where there was nothing in his way. But then this "boundary," or whatever it was, was gone. And when the watchman had recovered his wits, he continued his rounds, his head lowered in thought, his hands clasped behind him, and his steps now sculpted by his growing determination to discover what and where this boundary was.

As fate would have it though, a stray dog was the first to find this border zone and ascertain that it was made from the empty stares of those who wash and gargle when they rise interlarded with their lingering awareness of the persistence of the previous night's dream logic coupled with the echoes that reverberate from the shards of broken glass with which we crown our residential walls.

躍場

滿鋪靜謐的山路的轉彎處，一輛放空的出租轎車，緩緩地，不自覺地停了下來。那個年輕的司機忽然想起這空曠的一角叫「躍場。」『是啊，躍場』於是他又想及怎麼是上和怎麼是下的問題——他有點模糊了；以及租賃的問題『是否靈魂也可以出租…？』

而當他載著乘客複次經過那裏時，突然他將車猛地剎停而俯首在方向盤上哭了；他以為他已經撞燬了剛才停在那裏的那輛他現在所駕駛的車，以及車中的他自己。

The Turnabout

At a turn in a mountain road paved in silence, a taxi cab rolls to a gradual stop, as if of its own accord. The young driver, in the otherwise empty cab, has suddenly recalled that this desolate spot is referred to as "The Turnabout." Repeating the name aloud to himself, he reflects yet again on how it is we know that one is up, another down, one ahead, another far behind, at which point his thoughts—he is indeed a bit lost—alight upon a question for the leasing industry: "If a man has mortgaged his soul, what then?"

Later, passing the same spot, this time with passengers in the cab, the driver suddenly slams on the brakes and, pressing his brow against the steering wheel, he falls to weeping at the conviction that he has just plowed into his own cab while it was parked there earlier and he, still at the wheel.

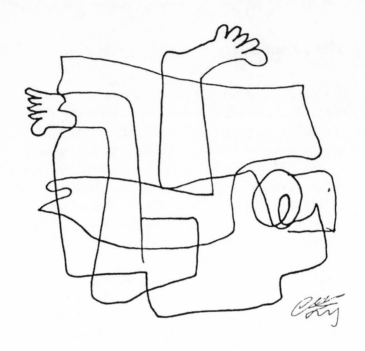

木星

窗子那面的爐灶旁，在滾動著的地球的后面，
天空是落寞的媽媽的眼睛。雲在發炎。菜鏟子
舞動著，聲響是受驚的鳥從熱鍋中飛起。而且
一個小孩在一瞬間長高；一隻剛剛從午夢中醒
來，因為咬不著自己的尾巴而不斷旋轉的是黃
狗亦是木星。

Jupiter

Near the stove by the window over there, on the far side of the tumbling earth, the sky is the eye of a forlorn mother. The clouds have become inflamed. A garden hoe breaks into dance with the sound of a startled bird bolting from a hot skillet. Likewise, a child experiences a growth spurt. And the creature that just awoke from the dream of an afternoon and is now whirling in circles in the fruitless effort to bite its own tail is both a yellow dog and the planet Jupiter.

溺酒的天使

酒瓶跌破之後，那飲者不但爲芳香四溢的液體之迸流而嘆息，且頹然地匍匐在地上，囁嚅地說：「你並沒有罪啊，正如我是一樣。爲什麼呢，不當心嗎？別人都喜歡綠色的天堂，而你鄙棄一朵臃腫的菊花──誠然，它那樣子真蠢──但我是無能幫助你了，我已經微醺。」因爲一個天使正溺在他自己所碰翻的酒中──或是他方自盛酒的瓶中溢出亦未可知──他半透明的黃色的小膀翅正被淺綠色的液體溶化著…
「也好。」飲者說：「同我一樣，做一個真正的人吧。」那聲音高得祗有瞎眼的老鼠和未滿月的嬰兒才能聽得見。

The Drunken Angel

When the bottle fell and shattered on the floor, the barfly did not just sigh over the spilt wine that filled the air with its perfume, but got down on his hands and knees and wept, muttering, "You're no more guilty than I am. What wayward step has brought you to this? The entire world adores a verdant heaven but you scorn the gravid chrysanthemum. To be sure, it behaved like a bonehead, but what can I do? I'm more than a little befuddled myself." Just then he noticed the gossamer yellow wings of a tiny angel struggling to keep from drowning in the wine that had spilled from the bottle it had knocked over, or had in fact been trapped in—it was most difficult to tell which—were beginning to dissolve in the pale green liquid. "Perhaps it's for the best," said the barfly. "Now maybe you'll become a real human being like me." But the sound of his voice was pitched so high only a blind mouse or a newborn infant could have heard a single word he said.

阿米巴弟弟

拉著我草綠色衣角的小孩，哭打著從樓梯上
退下來的阿米巴弟弟，對他的邀請我支吾地
拒絕了。這簡直是一隻噪月的獸，他的頸子
說：爲什麼不到樓上我的家去？那時你看見
梯子，又細又長，你在城裡有一個窩和一些
星子嗎？

我奇怪人有一個這樣的弟弟「是既乾淨又髒
的？」像一隻手，浣熊的，我想其掌心一定
像穿山甲的前爪。一個人有個阿米巴弟弟既
像浣熊又像穿山甲，而我在夜半的街頭有數
十個影子。

My Amoeba Kid Brother

After Joan Miró's "Dog Barking at the Moon"

The angry little fellow plucking at my khaki shirttail as I
barrel down the stairs is my amoeba kid-brother, whose
invitation I only managed to turn down after endless
hemming and hawing. The boy is an absolute beast, a dog
barking at the moon. The scruff of his neck whines, "How
come you never wanna come up to my place? You saw the
ladder, look how long and narrow it is. You got a nest of
your own in town like this, with stars?"

Weird how anyone could have a kid brother like that,
"clean and dirty at the same time." Like a hand or the paw
of a raccoon. I bet the underside of that paw is the spitting
image of a pangolin's front footpad. So a guy has an amoeba
kid-brother who simultaneously resembles a raccoon and a
pangolin, while I throw scores of shadows on the midnight
streets.

烤鵝

一隻剛烤好的全鵝飛走了。並且，攫去我們僅有的一瓶特級清酒。在一個晴朗的月夜，一朵將萎的茼蒿菊似地我們赤裸裸地俯身在海濱的沙灘上，唱著：『不用金屬的刀和叉。也不使竹筷的，我們是一群啜瓶口的酒徒喲！我們是吃「美」的饕餮者。啊！你黃油油的香噴噴的一隻新烤的全鵝呀！你黃油油的香噴噴的一隻新烤的全鵝呀⋯』直到晨霧將我們神聖的裸體輕掩，露珠自我們發紅的鼻尖滴下⋯

Roasted Goose

A fully roasted goose flew off, straight from the oven. On top of that, it decamped with our only bottle of premium saké. On a fine moonlit night, our bodies bent like withered mums, we stood naked on the sandy shores of the sea, singing: "We don't use no silverware. You won't catch us with bamboo chopsticks. Gluttons for 'beauty,' we imbibe our brew straight from the bottle. O roasted goose, so buttery and fragrant! O roasted goose, so buttery ..." and so on till the morning mist had veiled our sacred flesh and the dewdrops pearled from the tips of our beet-red noses.

冷藏的火把

深夜停電飢餓隨黑暗來襲，點一支臘燭去冰
箱尋找果腹的東西。正當我打開冰箱覓得自
己所要的事物之同時突然發現：燭光，火焰
珊瑚般紅的，煙長髮般黑的，祇是，唉，它
們已經凍結了。正如你揭開你的心胸，發現
一支冷藏的火把。

The Frozen Torch

Late last night when a power outage threw the whole house into darkness, I was suddenly seized by a terrific urge to eat. Lighting a candle I went into the kitchen and had no sooner opened the refrigerator door and started rummaging about than I discovered that the candlelight, both the coral-red flame and the hair-like strands of black smoke, had turned, alas, to ice. It was just as if I'd opened up your chest and found a frozen torch.

楓

一個小孩指著路旁的一株樹問我：「這是什麼樹？」

那時是三月。我說：「樹。」

樹的枝幹都呈銀灰色，嫩綠的葉片像那個小孩的小手；但是，他不滿意於我的答覆，他生氣了，歪著脖子嚷道：「樹？是什麼樹呀！」我怎麼能告訴他哩，那時是三月。我說：「小朋友，你還小——你幾歲呀？」

「六歲半。」他說。

「好。」我拍拍他的長著細長的毛髮的頭說：「過半年，等你滿七歲我告訴你。」

像游過一個小小的池塘，六個月後，楓樹們都露出鵝一樣紅色的腳距在風中舞弄。但是，紡織娘和叫哥哥奪去了那小孩對我的友誼——他不再來問我這是什麼樹了？

一天傍晚，我從樹下拾起一片猩紅的葉子來，向一個正從我身旁走過的老人說：「這是一片楓葉哦。」

那老人，用一種秋天的草原特有的眼神狠狠地看了我一眼說：「我知道！」然後隨著那被西風捲起的葉群氣虎虎地走了…

Maple

A little boy pointed to a tree by the side of the road and said, "What kind of tree is that?"

This was back in March, so I replied, "It's a *tree* tree."

The trunk and branches were silvery gray and its tender leaves were just like the hands of the little boy, but for some reason my answer failed to please him. Twisting his face in anger, he shrieked, "A *tree* tree? What kind of tree is that?" But what could I say? After all, it was March. "You're still so young, my little friend," I said. "How old are you anyway?" "Six and a half," he replied.

"Excellent," I said and gave him a pat on the crown of his fleecy head. "Come back in six months when you're seven and I'll tell you."

Six months passed as if they'd sailed across a small pond. The maples bared their webbed feet, as red as any goose's, and let them waggle in the wind, but the katydids and katydidn'ts must have set the boy's heart against me for he never once came back to ask me the name of that tree.

But then one evening I picked up a scarlet leaf that had fallen from the tree and, turning to an old man who chanced to be passing by, said, "This is a maple leaf."

"I know!" he snapped, glaring at me with the withering look of a prairie in autumn and then stormed off into the swirl of leaves borne away by the west wind.

手套

有一次，我在做完工後，回到寢室裏，先脫下一隻手套，向床上一扔；然後，掏出一支香菸來唧在嘴上，並且，已擦燃了火柴，正準備吸時，忽然，我從火焰尖端的黑煙燻飄中透過，凝視著那隻躺在床上的被黃土染黃了的黑土染黑了的被黃土和黑土染成了赭褐的白粗的手套。

此刻，那隻手套，因離了我的手，自然是空癟的；食指成三十度地斜曲著，小指被疊壓在無名指和中指之下，已看不見，甚至，簡直像斷了一個指頭。呵，它是如何地充滿了孤獨的哀傷之情。我急急撳滅了火柴，把另一隻手套脫下來，很快地丟在它旁邊。

第二隻手套，卻是仰臥著的。手指都無力地攤開來，指尖向著原先那隻，距離約十公分成為一個直角；說是休息著哩卻又煞像哆嗦；就這樣，一雙赭褐色的粗白色手套，唉，再也沒有比這更能象徵出：沒有希望的希望，絕對的空虛的悲哀，與千萬萬分的頹廢的人。即使是一個未亡人擁一襲外套跳慢板的華爾滋。

The Gloves

Once, when I had called it a day and gone back to my room, I pulled off one of my work gloves and tossed it on the bed so I could fish out a cigarette and light up, but I had no sooner struck a match and was on the point of inhaling when I found myself staring through the smoke of the match flame at the coarse cotton glove, once white but now stained yellow by yellow earth, black by black earth, and dingy ocher where black and yellow earth had mixed.

Without my hand to fill it, the glove had, quite naturally, collapsed upon itself, with its index finger bent at a thirty-degree angle and its pinkie, which lay crumpled beneath the ring- and middle-fingers, all but invisible to the point that it looked exactly as if the glove were missing a finger. It grieved me to think how lonely it must feel at that moment, and so I quickly shook out the match, tore off the other glove, and tossed it on the bed beside the first glove.

But the second glove just lay there on its back, its fingers splayed in exhaustion, inertly pointing in the direction of the other glove, which lay at a right angle to the first some ten centimeters away. You might think the gloves were only resting, but they were in fact shivering, which left me sighing at the thought that nothing could more symbolize hope without hope, sorrow without significance, or the thousands upon thousands of lost souls at the nth degree of their decrepitude than a pair of soiled white work gloves. Not even a widow dancing a slow waltz with an empty overcoat.

玩笑

有一次，我和一群螞蟻開了一個不小的玩笑。

盛夏的驟雨初停，空氣異樣的清新。一群螞蟻正忙碌於建造牠們的新居。每一隻螞蟻都非常勤奮有從地穴中掘出一小粒的黃土，啣來拋在穴外一公分半遠的地方；而那些小小的黃土粒，很快就堆成一道小小的圍牆。牠們似乎都很高興。但是，我和牠們開了一個不小的玩笑。

我把一隻出外尋找食物的螞蟻捉住，用手指輕輕將牠捻殺；然後，從牠們新築的巢穴之上空丟下；丟在那道小小圍堵當中的那些正在慶祝牠們又完成一片領土的征服的蟻群中。我看見那些素以勇敢，團結著名的螞蟻，忽然變得非常地怯懦，自私起來了；僅一秒鐘的時間還不到，便都逃得精光。可是，我卻只是和自己開了一個玩笑。當我把那隻捻死了的螞蟻的屍體從空中丟下之時，我好像聽見一個巨靂似的聲音從每隻螞蟻的口中驚呼出來；而我就是把這聲音投到自己心中的人。那聲音說：「啊，死！」

也許這在牠們，是唯一的宗教問題。

可是，我總是和自己開了一個很大的玩笑。

The Joke

I once played a joke on a colony of ants.

It was on one of those sultry summer days when a sudden downpour leaves the air clean and fresh that I chanced upon the ants just as they were constructing a new nest. It looked as though the entire colony had thrown itself into the task, for ant after ant emerged from the nest with a little grain of yellow earth clasped between its jaws and dropped it a few centimeters from the nest entrance. In no time at all the little grains had grown into a tiny protective wall. The ants seemed very happy. That is, until I played my not-so-little joke.

Noticing an ant leaving the nest on a foraging expedition, I swept it up with my hand and crushed it lightly between my fingers, then, holding it directly above the nest entrance where the ants were just then gathering to congratulate themselves on having colonized yet another corner of the earth, I let it go. It struck me how these creatures, so famous for their courage and group loyalty, fled in horror at the mere sight of the dead ant falling among them. In less than a second they had all vanished.

But the joke was on me. For at the very moment I dropped the dead ant, I seemed to hear a thunderous cry escape from the mouth of every ant in the colony, a cry I have since taken very much to heart: "O, death!"

For all I know this is their one religious notion. Be that as it may, the joke is still on me.

狗

每次，當我從欄柵式的木板窗縫中望出去，一直把這條臨河的，還不怎麼成其為街的路看到黃昏。一直把那盞不知從何時起點著的路燈，由昏黃看到明亮。一直看到那個遛狗的人出現在路燈的照射之下。

每次，總是要等到那個人快接近路燈時，才看得見一隻灰灰的狗，跟在他的後面；他人愈近燈桿，那黑黑的狗靠他也更近，人一到燈下，那狗便不見了，我想大概是翹著腿在燈桿下做了什麼了；可是當他一走過燈桿，那狗就突然越過人而跑到了他的前面，愈走愈遠，直到人從燈光中消失。

一個人擁有這樣一隻忠實而有趣的狗。是多麼令人羨慕啊。

直到有一天，我禁不住想要和那人去打個招呼，而走出了我的小木屋；當我走向那盞路燈時，我才發現，我也有一隻忠實的狗跟在我後面，並且也在我走過燈桿之後急急的跑在我的前面，愈跑愈遠，終於消失在沒有燈光之處。

Dog

Every time I peer out through the louvered window my eye is caught by the lane—you can hardly call it a street—that runs along the river, and I wind up staring out until evening falls and the street lamp I never seem to notice coming on grows bright, and the man with the gray dog appears in its circle of light.

Odd how I never see the dog until the man has almost reached the street lamp, when it suddenly appears at his heels and scurries to overtake him, which it does just as the man is passing the light but then it disappears—no doubt to lift a leg against the lamppost—then reappears again, only this time in front, then races on ahead faster and faster until it vanishes from the circle of light.

The man who owns such a trusty and interesting dog is indeed to be envied.

Things go on like this for quite some time until one day, overcome by an irresistible urge to say hello to the man, I venture from my little wooden hut and walk toward the street lamp to wait for him. But no sooner have I approached the lamp than I discover that I too have a trusty dog at my heels, which scurries to overtake me just as I pass the lamppost, then races on ahead faster and faster until at last it disappears in the darkness.

音速

悼王迎先

有人從橋上跳下來。

那姿勢零亂而僵直，恰似電影中道具般的身
軀，突然，在空中，停格了1/2秒，然后才
緩緩繼續下降。原來，他被從水面反彈回來
的自己在蹤身時所發出的那一聲淒厲的叫喊
托了一下，因而在落水時也祇有淒楚一響。

The Speed of Sound

*An elegy for Wang Yingxian, "drowned" in police
custody, May 7, 1982*

Someone leapt from a bridge.

As he was falling through the air, his body as stiff and
disjointed as a prop dummy in a B movie, he suddenly
stopped, a full half-second, before resuming his long free
fall. The truth is that the force of his scream rebounding
off the surface of the water had momentarily arrested his
momentum. Which also goes a long way toward explaining
why he made such a pitiful splash.

月光

悼或人

根據一位目擊者的描述,說:開始時我簡直被他的行徑所震驚,他舉步在微風中搖擺著的芒草之頂端,他難道是達摩?他又高舉手杖兩臂向外猛揮,彷彿在叱吒著什麼,他大概以為自己是能叫海水讓路的摩西,雖然溪水很淺,然而隨處都有盜探砂石所留下的坑洞,不過,我沒有聽到任何水聲,已經是十六號凌晨,月亮特別圓,天空非常藍,按理他可以抵達彼岸。

他的衣褲甚至鞋子都沒有打濕。根據法醫的報告:他是被月光淹死的。

Moonlight

For someone

One eyewitness described the incident as follows: "At first I was simply bowled over, I mean the guy was walking right across the tips of the reeds as they were waving in the wind. So I'm thinking to myself, 'Is he the Bodhidharma or what?' But then he raises his staff above his head with both hands and starts thrashing the air like he was trying to break someone to his will. Guess he thought he was Moses commanding the waters to part. The brook is pretty shallow to be sure, but there are some deep hollows where they've quarried for sand. Still, I don't recall the sound of anything falling in the water, and it was nearly dawn by then. This was on the 16th. The moon was incredibly bright and the sky was this intense blue, so I don't see any reason why he shouldn't have made it to the other shore."

There was no evidence that his shoes or clothing had come into contact with water on the night of the incident. "Death due to a surfeit of moonlight," was the conclusion of the coroner.

火燄

(馬善疑點)

每當西風走過，每當暗夜，每當鼻塞，每當
獨行，僅管我的步伐依然穩健，卻爲何我的
身影總是忽明忽滅？

遂想起那年，他們在打斷了整綑扁担之后，
竟捨棄刀槍不用而改以一壺冷水灌進我的鼻
孔我的嘴巴，直到我停息了漫罵。

難道，他們那時就已經得知，我的生命本是
一團火燄，是一盞從古佛殿前逃亡的明燈？

The Flame

(The Curious Incident of Ma Shan)

Whenever the west wind blows, whenever the evening darkness gathers, whenever my nose is stuffed, whenever I walk alone, why is it that my shadow always flickers even though my stride is no less firm than it was before?

I find myself thinking back to that fateful year they broke half a dozen bamboo poles across my back, then, having realized the futility of conventional instruments of persuasion, flushed my throat and nostrils with icy water until they finally succeeded in staunching my curses.

Is it possible they could have realized even then that my life was originally a ball of fire, a candle flame that had bolted from the altar of an ancient Buddhist temple?

電鎖

這晚，我住的那一帶的路燈又準時在午夜停電了。

當我在掏鑰匙的時候，好心的計程車司機趁倒車之便把車頭對準我的身後，強烈的燈光將一個中年人濃黑的身影毫不留情的投射在鐵門上，直到我從一串鑰匙中選出了正確的那一支對準我心臟中的部位插進去，好心的計程車司機才把車開走。

我也才終於將插在我心臟中的鑰匙輕輕的轉動了一下「咔」，隨即把這段靈巧的金屬從心中拔出來順勢一推斷然的走了進去。

沒多久我便習慣了其中的黑暗。

The Lock Electric

On this night, as always, the street-lamps in the district where I live went out at midnight.

As I was fishing for my keys, the kindly cabby kept his headlights trained in my direction as he backed down the drive. In the glare of the headlights the thick black shadow of a middle-aged man was ruthlessly silhouetted against the iron door until, that is, I finally found the key on the chain, aimed it just about the place my heart was and thrust it in, whereupon the kindly cabby turned and drove away.

And so I gave the key a gentle *click*, drew out the ingenious sliver of metal, and in one fluid motion thrust the door open and boldly stepped inside.

I soon grew used to the darkness within.

穿牆貓

自從她離去之後便來了這隻貓，在我的住處進出自如，門窗乃至牆壁都擋牠不住。

她在的時候，我們的生活曾令鐵門窗外的雀鳥羨慕，她照顧我的一切，包括停電的晚上為我捧來一鉤新月（她相信寫詩用不著太多的照明），燠熱的夏夜她站在我身旁散發冷氣。

錯在我不該和她討論關於幸福的事。那天，一反平時的吶吶，我說：「幸福，乃是人們未曾得到的那一半。」次晨，她就不辭而別。

她不是那種用唇膏在妝鏡上題字的女子，她也不用筆，她用手指用她長長尖尖的指甲在壁紙上深深的寫道：今後，我便成為你的幸福，而你也是我的。

自從這隻貓在我的住處出入自如以來，我還未曾真正的見過牠，牠總是，夜半來，天明去。

The Cat That Walks Through Walls

Ever since she left me some cat's been coming in and out of my apartment as if it owns the place—locked doors, grated windows, even walls can't seem to stop it.

When she was still with me the very sparrows outside the iron gate were green with envy, for she catered to my each and every need. On evenings when the power failed she would even bring me the new moon with the old moon in its arms (she did not believe that writing poetry required much light), and on hot summer nights would stand beside my bed exuding her cool airs.

My mistake came in broaching the subject of human happiness. In contrast to my usual loss for words, I blurted, "Happiness is the half that people never get." The next morning she left without saying a word.

She was not the kind of woman to leave a message scrawled in lipstick on her vanity mirror. She didn't even use a pen. Instead, with her long, sharp fingernails she scratched these words deep into the wallpaper: "From this day forth, I shall be your happiness, as you shall be mine."

Although I can't keep this cat from invading my apartment, I haven't actually seen it yet, for it never comes until the wee hours of the night, and always leaves before first light.

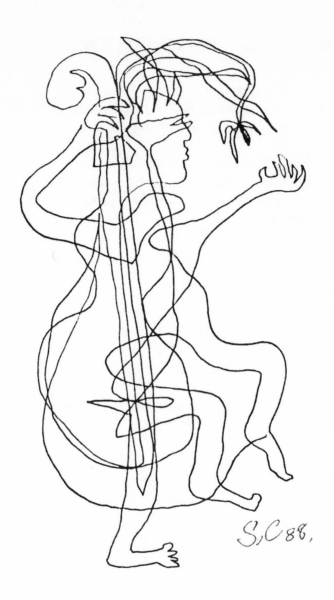

頭七

紀念女兒她們母親的母親

都快到家了。

當她以半世紀前的習慣，俯身在這條少女時代浣衣的溪畔，發現雙手竟然捧不起半點清涼，而平如明鏡的水面照不出她絲毫的形影；這才想起兒媳們都作興上教堂，沒有人為她唸經，她連一塊靈牌都沒有。

一瓣桃花從月牙上流過，外婆差一點哭出聲來。她幾乎忘了自己是踏著茅草的波浪踏著蘆花的波浪踏著台灣海峽的波浪踏著洞庭湖的波浪回來的。

The First Week of Mourning

In memory of my daughters' mother's mother

Nearly home.

When, true to the habits of half a century, she bent down by the brook where she had washed her clothes as a child and discovered, much to her surprise, that she could not scoop up even half a drop of its refreshing clarity or see the slightest sign or shadow of her reflection in the mirror-like surface of the water, then, and only then, did she recall that because her son and daughter-in-law had followed the fashion of going to Church, no one had bothered to chant a Buddhist sutra to ease her soul into the next world, much less honor her in this world by giving her a spirit tablet in the family shrine.

As a peach petal floats through the fangs of the crescent moon, grandma almost bursts into tears. She has all but forgotten how she had just walked upon the waves of couch grass and walked upon the waves of rush flowers and walked upon the waves of the Formosa Strait and walked upon the waves of Dongting Lake and is nearly home.

1987

三七

紀念孩子們的大舅父

爲了解釋他並非死於間諜，他又急急地來到
我的窗前，他身上殘餘的海灘氣味還激怒了
屋角上那隻懶洋洋的暹邏貓。

爲了解釋並非死於預謀，他只能把變幻莫測
的洋流溫度傳到我的身上，害得我在睡夢中
忽冷忽熱。可憐他早已失去了人世的語言。

爲了解釋他如何被一個海流漩渦以及海草所
吸納，他恁由自己浮動的魄影被窗簾圍繞復
圍繞，在我猶未驚醒之前緩緩沉入又黑又深
的天空。

The Third Week of Mourning

In memory of the children's eldest uncle

In order to explain that he had not in fact been executed for spying, he lost no time in returning to my window, where, as always, the faint odor of seaside that perpetually hung about him infuriated the Siamese cat lolling in its corner of the roof.

In order to explain that he had not in fact been the victim of a conspiracy, he attempted to convey to me, by bodily transfer, the fickle temperature changes of the ocean currents, thereby disrupting my sleep with hot and cold flashes. Sadly, he had lost the power of speech.

In order to explain how he had been dragged down by the swirling eddies and strands of sea grass, he allowed the shadow of his unfettered soul to become entangled in fold after fold of the window curtain, but by the time my terror had awakened me, he had, by slow degrees, already sunk into the deep dark sky.

1988

五七

紀念孩子們的外公

聽罷比他早走數年至今尤是孤魂野鬼的部屬
有著每被芝麻大小的神祇所爲難而不能盡收
生前足跡的抱怨之後，他不禁大嘆連靈界亦
充滿了勢利眼。要不，怎麼自己進入老家舊
宅院時並未受到任何攔阻。

而他生前的副官卻另有解釋，他說：長官，
回煞不順非關我的階級大小，問題出在我腿
中的那顆彈頭，雖然它生前以不同程度的痠
痛使我預知風雨，如今卻被自家的門神視爲
帶有凶器而不准進出。

現在，他終於諒解兒媳們將他火化並非忤逆
不孝了。記得撿骨的時候還有個孫子誤把熔
化後他脊椎旁那些彈片當作勳章哩。

The Fifth Week of Mourning

In memory of the children's maternal grandfather

When he had finished listening to the complaints of a subordinate who had passed away several years earlier than himself but was still forced to wander the empty fields and byways on account of the abuse he had to suffer from even the most menial of spirits whenever he ventured to return to his former haunts, the commander could not help but lament aloud that snobbery must be as rampant in the spirit world as it is in the world of the living. Why else was he himself allowed to come and go without the slightest hindrance?

But the subordinate, an aide-de-camp in their previous plane of existence, cast a rather different light upon the situation: "Commander," he said, "it is not my rank they object to but the bullet in my thigh. In life it allowed me to predict the weather with remarkable accuracy on account of the varying degrees of discomfort I felt, but here it only seems to make the door gods standing watch over my former residence treat me as though I were harboring a dangerous weapon. Thus do they prevent me from coming and going."

Thus the commander finally understood that his son and daughter-in-law had been neither disobedient nor disrespectful in having him cremated, and recalled how when his family had gathered to collect his ashes one of his grandsons had even mistaken the melted shell splinters that had lodged themselves near his spine for the remnants of a campaign medal.

1988

雪

我把一頁信紙從反面摺疊。這樣比較白幸好
那人不愛兩面都寫。疊了又疊,再斜疊,成
一個錐形。再用一把小剪刀來剪,又剪又挖,
然後

我老是以為,雪是這樣造成的:把剪好的信
紙展開來,還好,那人的字跡纖細一點也不
會透過來,白的,展開,六簇的雪花就攤在
臘黃的手掌上。然而

在三千公尺或者更高的空中,一群天使面對
下界一個大廣場上肢體的狼藉,手足無措,
而氣溫突然降至零度以下,他們的爭辯與嗟
嘆逐漸結晶而且紛紛飄墜。

Snow, June 1989

I fold the letter from the back, that way it's whiter and
thank my lucky stars the man doesn't like to write on both
sides. Fold it in half, and half again cattycorner till it forms
a wedge. Get out my little pair of scissors, snip it here, snip
it there, and poke out all the pieces, then

I've always thought that this is just the way they make the
snow, and so unfold the little fellow—isn't it nice he writes
so lightly not a single word shows through—when Voila!
One snowy six-point snowflake sprawled on my withered
yellow palm, but

At 10,000 feet or even higher, a chorus of angels is all in a
dither at seeing the bodies that litter the great public square,
when out of the blue the temperature falls and all of their
quarrels and all of their sighs begin to crystallize until one
by one they fall.

雞

星期天，我坐在公園中靜僻的一角一張缺腿
的鐵凳上，享用從速食店買來的午餐。啃著
啃著，忽然想起我已經好幾十年沒有聽過雞
叫了。

我試圖用那些骨骼拼成一隻能夠呼喚太陽的
禽鳥。我找不到聲帶。因爲牠們已經無須啼
叫。工作就是不斷的進食，而牠們生產牠們
自己。

在人類製造的日光下
既沒有夢
也沒有黎明

Domestic Fowl

Sunday found me sitting in a quiet corner of the park on an iron bench, which happened to be missing a leg, enjoying my fast food lunch, when, munching away, it occurred to me I hadn't heard a rooster crow in years.

So I ventured to piece the leftover bones into this "feathered biped that can summon the sun," but I couldn't find its vocal cords. No doubt because roosters no longer need to crow. Now all these creatures ever do is eat, and their sole labor is to produce themselves.

Under a man-made sun
There are neither dreams
Nor dawns

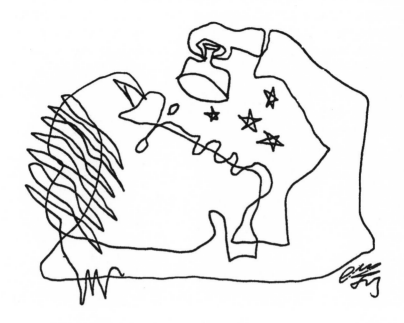

Translator's Notes

Feelings Above Sea Level

The Chinese text reads "Indian prince" rather than "Kashmiri prince." I've made the change to avoid possible confusion with the Indians of North and South America. Similarly, I added the phrase "at Fangshan Dinglin Temple" to "nippled bell" 乳鐘 (*ruzhong*) so as to avoid confusion with "nipple bell," which could hardly be further from the meaning and import of the original, a famous bell at the Fangshan Dinglin Temple in China purportedly adorned with 180 nipple-shaped ornaments.

Border Zone

The illustration accompanying this prose poem was made by the poet at the Poetry International Festival Rotterdam 2002, to which he was invited, during a translation work-shop that was translating (among other things) this poem, in order to shed light on the significance of the title 界 (*Jye*), which could be interepreted as "boundary," "margin," "border," "territory," and even "world," both real and imagined. Taking my cue from the martial subtext suggested by the first line of the poem as well as the drawing, I have translated the word as "Border Zone" in the title and as "boundary" where it occurs in the poem proper. Until recently, it was a common practice in Taiwan to line the tops of residential walls with shards of broken glass to keep off the pigeons and keep out the cat burglars.

My Amoeba Kid Brother

With Shang Qin's approval, I have added the descriptive epigraph, which is not included in the original poem. This painting, as Michelle Yeh has pointed out in a 1996 article on the poet titled, "'Variant Keys' and 'Omni Vision': A Study of Shang Qin" (*Modern Chinese Literature* 9: 327-367, 342), is one of Shang Qin's favorites and the subject of a free verse poem written in 1942 by the Taiwanese modernist poet Ji Xian 紀弦.

Maple

Where I have "katydids and katydidn'ts" the Chinese text reads "Weaving Maid" 紡織娘 (*fangzhi niang*) and "Call Me Older Brother" 叫哥哥 (*jiao gege*), which are Chinese colloquial terms for (respectively) a grasshopper whose call resembles the sound of a weaver's shuttle, and a species of the katydid. I used the term "katydidn'ts" to draw attention to the presence, if not substance, of Shang Qin's word play.

The Speed of Sound

Wang Yingxian was illegally detained and tortured on suspicion of being involved in a 1982 bank robbery, the first in Taiwanese history. According to police reports, Wang, who signed a confession admitting to involvement in the crime, escaped during a prison transfer, threw himself off a bridge, and was drowned. However, many Taiwanese believe the police, who were under great pressure to solve the crime, may have murdered him in an attempt to extract a confession. Whatever the case, the incident became a national scandal and helped prompt the courts to end their long indifference to police brutality under the then martial-law rule of the Nationalist party.

Moonlight

As I noted in my preface, this 1987 poem is awash with allusions to Max Jacob's prose poem "The Truly Miraculous," which, in William T. Kulik's English, runs thus: "Our dear old priest! After he'd left us, we saw him flying over the lake like a bat. He was so absorbed in his thoughts he didn't even see the miracle. He was astonished to find the hem of his cassock was wet" (*Dreaming the Miracle, Three French Prose Poets: Jacob, Ponge, Follain*, Buffalo, New York: White Pine Press, 2003: 28). It is also worth noting that Shang Qin's use of the phrase "the other shore" is quite ironic, in that it is a well-known Buddhist trope for "the next world."

The Flame

This poem, as Shang Qin notes in a recent interview in *Fascicle*, is based in part on personal experience and in part on the character named in the poem's parenthetical epigraph, a general in the Ming novel *The Investiture of the Gods (Feng Shen Bang)* who could not be injured because he had once been a candle flame in a temple altar.

The Cat That Walks Through Walls

Shang Qin was married for a time to the poet Luo Ying 羅英 (1940-). Two daughters resulted from the marriage.

Snow, June 1989

This poem was written in response to the Tiananmen Square Massacre and is remarkable for its indirectness. Indeed, it is so indirect that I have felt obliged to add the phrase "June 1989" to its title, which is simply "Snow" in the original, to ensure that the poem's informing context, so obvious to Shang Qin's Taiwanese readers, is not lost on readers unfamiliar with the Chinese language, culture, and political history. For those who grew up in East Asia, and for Chinese everywhere, almost any reference to a large public square "littered with bodies" invariably suggests the image of Beijing's Tiananmen Square on the fateful night of June 3, 1989, when the Chinese Communist leadership, infuriated by the pro-democracy protestors refusal to end their highly publicized seven-week vigil, ordered the People's Liberation Army to make the protestors leave the square by any means necessary. Escorted by tanks and armored vehicles, thousands of armed troops converged upon the "Gate of Heavenly Peace" and indiscriminately fired upon protesters and bystanders alike, killing hundreds, and possibly thousands, of unarmed civilians. Small wonder the angels in Shang Qin's prose poem are thrown into such a "dither."

Similarly, for readers familiar with the Chinese literary tradition, almost any allusion to a heaven-sent snow in the month of June is bound to call to mind the popular Beijing opera "June Snow" 六月雪 (*Liuyue xue*), which recounts the story of a young woman wrongly accused of murder, who, in the middle of June, on the eve of her execution, vows that it will snow at the moment of her death as "Heaven's proof of her innocence." When snow does fall immediately after she is publicly executed, the magistrate in charge of the case is moved to reverse his decision, whereupon he takes steps to seek out and punish the guilty and to appease the spirit of the wronged woman. Shang Qin's poem can thus be read as both an indictment of the actions of the Chinese government and a prayer for the dead.

Although origami may seem a rather oblique and emotionally detached way to memorialize those who died in Tiananmen Square, it is neither when seen in the interpreting light of the poet's informing traditions. Not only is white the funereal color throughout East Asia, it has long been a practice at Chinese funerals to burn fake paper money folded in half or in the shape of silver ingots to underwrite the spirit's journey to and sojourn in the next world. At the same time, as psychologists have long pointed out, mechanically creative tasks such as origami can be psychologically comforting to the bereaved. I am reminded in particular of the origami cranes that thousands of children in Japan and elsewhere make each year in memory of Sadako Sasaki, the "child of the atomic bomb" who died in a Red Cross hospital before she had time to finish folding the thousand paper cranes that a pre-nuclear folk wisdom believed would save her from the leukemia she had contracted on the morning of August 6, 1945, when "the sky flashed white" over the city of Hiroshima. Like the millions of white paper cranes that are rained upon the Hiroshima Peace Park on the anniversary of the atomic bomb, the folding of a "white six-point snowflake" in memory of those who died in Tiananmen Square is a poignant response to a most painful episode in the modern history of state-sanctioned violence.

Domestic Fowl

This poem has been translated by Michelle Yeh, Göran Malmqvist, and others as "Rooster," but the Chinese title 雞 (Ji) is the common generic term for chicken as well as rooster. As both genders figure prominently in the poem, with Shang Qin's approval, I have opted for the more general term "Domestic Fowl," which introduces a pun not conveyed by the original title.

List of Drawings

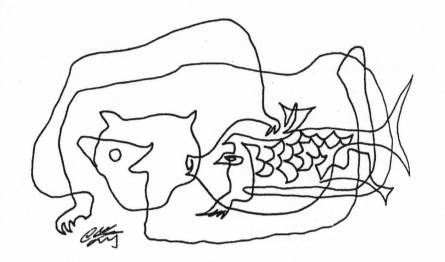

Shang Qin (Shang Ch'in) was born in China in 1930, but has lived in Taiwan since 1950. The author of four volumes of verse, he is among the first poets in Taiwan to have expressed a significant interest in surrealism and is the finest poet on either side of the Formosa Strait to have made the prose poem his métier. His poetry has been translated into English, Dutch, French, German and Swedish.

Steve Bradbury is Associate Professor of English at National Central University in Taiwan. He has published poems, translations, and essays in *Jacket, Raritan, Tinfish* and many other journals. Zephyr Press also publishes his *Fusion Kitsch: Poems from the Chinese of Hsia Yü* (2001).